Inside Out

Jade Castledine

BookLeaf Publishing
India | USA | UK

Presentation by *BookLeaf Publishing*

Web: www.bookleafpub.com

E-mail: info@bookleafpub.com

ISBN: 978-93-5744-438-5

First edition 2022

DEDICATION

To myself, and the journey of becoming me.

PREFACE

A collection of feelings from chapter 32; at a point in life which felt like mountain climbing. The unwritten poems became a source of healing... I just didn't know it.

I am Me

I wonder why we exist?
I hear how you think.
I see how you feel.
I want you to be free.
I am Me.

I pretend the world isn't crazy.
I feel angels exist.
I touch the moon within my soul.
I worry I have not done my bit.
I cry only when no-one is watching.
I am Me.

I understand that love heals all.
I say thank you each day.
I dream of making a difference.
I try my best each day.
I hope I fulfil the journey
I am Me.

Somethings

Somethings are good,
Somethings are bad,
and whatever makes you happy,
has the power to make you sad.

I am here

I am broken and bruised,
Alone and confused.
But I am here.

I am sad and distressed,
Worried and depressed.
But I am here.

I am numb and no fun,
Quiet and vulnerable.
But I am here.

I am stuck and trapped,
Can't remember when I last laughed.
But I am here.

I am love and light,
And won't give up the fight.
Because I am here.

The doorway

Hey,you!
Standing over there
YOU are in my doorway.

Her/She

Her heart is open:
she feels like the sunshine.

Her smile is worth gold:
she heals you without you knowing.

Her beauty is concealed:
she shows it only to those who earned it.

Her balance brings you strength:
she is peace.

You have not known her until…

You had been blessed with her presence
and felt her absence,

Received her love and lost her energy.

You won't know her until it's too late.

I am her and she is me

Six

The dark times aren't here to stay
Be patient and things will be fixed.
Just like granny would say "It won't always be
dark at six".

My dad

Today I feel so sad,
so sad I can not be mad
so sad I can not speak
so sad that I feel weak
and all I want is...

Love has no limits

The secret about love that you cannot explain
is when it is given or received it feels just the
same.

It reaches anywhere there is a connection
as true love has no opposite direction.

Listen with your heart you will understand
life is when love is found.

Impress Yourself

I'll be better today,
than yesterday,
and even more tomorrow.

The past has gone,
no need to dwell,
let it go and move on.

Who I was then,
is not who I am now,
nor who I will become.

Do it

Do afraid and then you'll be brave
Do it scared and then you'll be strong
Do it sad, do it mad and even after that you will
still be glad

VIP Blessed

you are Valued
 you are IMPORTANT
  you are PROTECTED

your **B**eautiful
 and **L**oved,
  Educated,
   Successful,
  keep **S**miling
  knowing **E**verything
   is **D**ivine

Patience

I fight back the tears
of the pain of the years
and still the voice I hear
whispers your time in near

Seasons

She was lost during winter.
She was found within the blossoms.
She grew under the sun.
She was changing like the leaves; she let go and
then was freed.

The little things

The stars in the blue sky when the sun is out.
Here shining, cheerleading – I am out of your
sight.

The stars on a cloudy day or those hidden by
moonlight. Here when it is dark - from a
distance you see my light.

The empty sky, you are lost and look for me.
Here to guide you - until you are happy.

Unnoticed in the sun I never went away.
The stars in the sky - here always.

Lessons

Strong enough to be vulnerable,
Wise enough not to judge,
The one who loves you warns you,
Keep hold of the lesson and the love.

Don't confuse the excitement with toxicity,
Listen when they speak,
Don't stay where you're not valued
To prove you deserve a seat.

The path you closed with fear,
can be opened with love.
Take it steady enjoy the ride.
Don't take on more than you should.

Let the boredom become the peace,
Bend in the wind.
Getting the best spot isn't easy,
All sadness comes to an end.

One thing to learn is that
short term pleasure never stays.
Gratitude makes happiness
- that is the real long term gain.

Thoughts and Desires

I am what I think
I am what I say
I am what I do

And within this moment
it feels as good as it looks too!

Happy Again

Lost
Immersed
Free of thought

Silent
Surrounded
A happy thought

Tingling
Smiling
Happy again

The one I never met

Mummy loved you
Mummy loves you
I did it because I wanted the best for you

I cry for you
I blame myself for you
Im angry I was not strong enough to

I miss you
I wish you could be here too
Im sorry I was too scared to

I sensed you
I'll be better for you
Mummy will always love you

The one who brought the Joy

Daughter
Cheeky and Clever
Loving, Smiling, Bossing
A Blessing

My Sunshine

The one who brought the love

There once was a little boy called Aziah
Whose love for animals was his only desire
He spent all his days - looking for creatures in
many ways
Who I actually wanted to call Zion

and now the joy of my life

The one who brought the knowledge

The funny one,
The happy one,
The clever, friendly, crazy one.

The first one,
The wild one,
The spontaneous, can be unpredictable one.

The different one,
The unique one,
The one who made the change

they'll see in time... we'll show them together

www.ingramcontent.com/pod-product-compliance
Lightning Source LLC
LaVergne TN
LVHW050248200726
843509LV00015B/2941